Back Alley Poems

Ken Greenley

Illustrated by Angela Mark
Photos by Chuck Svoboda

Published by Improbable Productions

Denver, Colorado

Copyright © 2017 Ken Greenley

All rights reserved.

ISBN: 0-9632326-4-9

ACKNOWLEDGMENTS

Poems from this book will appear in *Lummox* and *Big Hammer.* They can also be seen online at *OutlawPoetry.* I'd also like to thank Dave Roskos, John Richey, Mike Romoth, Chuck Svoboda, Barbara Test, Julie Cummings and Neil Kelly for encouraging me with my work and being the people they are. Also Matt Borkowski, Gregory Greyhawk and Lenny Chernilla for the help they gave me in the past. May they rest in peace. Thanks to my wife Vicki, for all that proofreading. And Michael Annis for technical support. I'd also like to thank the old Court Tavern in New Brunswick, New Jersey and Ziggie's Saloon and the Tattered Cover Bookstore in Denver, Colorado for being the type of places they are.

CONTENTS

Talk Like Your Dad	1
Character Actor	2
Free Thought	4
Your Own Eyes	6
Fences	8
Ya See That?	10
Without Jesse	13
Dr. King	15
Let Mystery Be	16
Dance	19
Jerry Rig	21
NYC Rat	23
Rat Rights	24
Back of the Bus of Death	26
Ken's Kangaroo Court	28
Of Crazy Horse and Christ	30
Three Stooges vs. PC	32
The McDali Lama	34
Fuckin Cosell	35
Cure	39
HMO Poem	41

Ahead of the Storms	43
To My Great Grandmother	44
Hurdler	47
Relay System	49
Crazy	51
No Shoelaces	52
Empath	54
Work that Sign, Bro	56
Old Man Role Models	58
Just Say Yeah	61
Bad Road Food	64
A Bird's Life	67
21st Century Elves	69
Bottles Don't Last	71
One More Won't Hurt	74
My Uncle and the Full Moon	76
Godspot	78
Them and their Tries	80

Flash Fiction

Doesn't Believe in Angels	85
Come to the Realization	90
Overtime in Omaha	95
The Old Riots	99
Playing in the DDT	106
Yifter the Shifter	110
Life, Death and Two Knuckleheads	116

Back Alley Poems

Talk Like Your Dad

Ya know how people say
you become more and more
like your Dad
the older you get?
Well, lately I've been talking like mine.
I've been here in Denver 20-odd years
And my New York accent has faded over time
But lately it's come back
As I talk more and more like my Dad
I don't know why
Happens when I've been drinking
Or when I feel threatened
or pissed off
Somehow it feels good again
to say get the hell outta heah
or fuggetabout it
Feels good to remember the sound of his voice
Especially that thick accent
It's very reassuring
Somehow I feel tougher
When I talk like my Dad.

Character Actor

So great
When a veteran character actor
Makes an appearance
Oh, it's that guy
I've seen him in a million movies
And I'm so glad to see him again
Like a long distance call from an old friend.

Can't be bad with this guy in it,
the best ones, the true chameleons
with faces like silly putty
So good an actor you can't tell who they are;
A different face for every role.
Guerilla actors
They come in, get the job done
and get out.

Going from movie to movie
Hardly mentioned, sometimes hardly noticed
If you're good with faces, not names
These are the guys for you.

'These guys'
with careers that last years and years
Fifty TV shows
Dozens of movies
Hundreds of roles under their belts
Like seasoning behind the movie,
that makes it taste so much better

Strange paradox
Famous but anonymous
Legions of them
Unsung
An army of familiar faces
with names we can't remember
Like unknown soldiers.

Free Thought

This started as a really cynical poem
About stupidity and how strong it is
How inexorable
But then I got to thinking
Free thought
Is one tough motherfucker too
Think of all it's been through
Consider the first free thinkers
What they must have endured
What are they doing?
Their fellow cave-men must have said
We're going on a hunt and there they are
Painting pictures inside a cave!
But that was just the beginning for free thought
Somehow it keeps right on rolling
In spite of everything
Think of the opposition it's faced
over the years
The Romans couldn't stop it
The Mongols couldn't stop it
The Inquisition couldn't stop it
The whole Victorian error couldn't stop it

Hitler couldn't stop it
Hollywood couldn't stop it
Nixon and his bunch couldn't stop it
And those Bushes they planted
They couldn't do a damn thing, either
Even now, here, in this place
A devil's alliance
between the media and the pentagon
Try to stamp out free thought every day
They've been trying for a while now
So far
All attempts have failed.

Your Own Eyes

JFK
9/11
Films exist
That clearly show
what the hell happened
Right in front of your eyes
Kennedy, the fatal shot
clearly fired from the front or side
Not from behind, like the warren commission said
9/11, the clips show
Black smoke from the jet fuel
billowing out from the tops of the towers
Then suddenly there's another explosion
far below that blows white smoke
out the middle of the buildings
Bringing the towers tumbling down
Collapsing right exactly in their own footprint
And oh yeah, they just happened to find
one of the hijackers' ID at the scene
Who would believe that?
Oh well, maybe you
And yes, we could argue

back and forth about this
till the cows come home
But one thing you can't dispute,
this government
doesn't want you
to believe your own eyes
Why?

Fences

Dividers between us
People say they make good neighbors
But they never say why
Markers of Possession
with big signs hung off them
that say KEEP OUT

That side's yours and this side's mine
Delineation, Demarcation
Enforcement of a boundary
Affirmation of lines on a map
The land parceled off, neat and clean
My yard, your yard
They're right in our own backyard!

Fences
They spring up across the country,
popping up everywhere, one after another
More and more open spaces and fenceless lots
disappearing
Always have, ever since the white man arrived
Ever since he fenced off the Range

with his telegraph lines and barbed wire
Dividing, slicing an ever-diminishing pie
As hundreds of millions of us pile up

Fences
We wish they weren't there
But what else would keep out wandering dogs?
Or the wandering people?
How else would we mark off our turf?
How else do we tell the world its ours?
Our little personal land area
Our piece

Fences, equalizers
Fences, facts on the ground
Death, Taxes and Fences
That's the way it is

Fences
More and more of them
Even though part of us
Doesn't really want them.

Ya See That?

Ya see that?

They did that

They always do shit like that

It's just the way they are

It's all they know

They're all fucked up

That is so typical of them.

Ya see that?

Words that birth contempt,

Codewords for intolerance

Rationalization

Justification

Dehumanization

Ya see that?

I was right about these guys

Right again

Solid, in the field evidence

Sums it all up

like Perry Mason in court

Guilty

Ya see that

Now it's OK to sneer at them,

to look down on them

to cop an attitude

To point the finger, to blame.

Ya see that?

They're the ones

They're the reason the neighborhood

is going to the dogs

They're the ones that throw garbage in the street

and tag the neighborhood walls with graffiti

and drive like assholes

They're the reason why it rains

or why it doesn't rain

They're everything that's wrong with the world today

Ya see that?

They ain't human anymore

Now we can hate them

Now we can ATTACK

Ya see that?

Without Jesse

Obama doesn't get there without Jesse Jackson
Jesse put it in peoples" minds first
Made what was unthinkable
Thinkable
Do-able
Jesse jumping right in the water
To learn how to swim
Jesse making it all possible
Obama doesn't get there without Jesse.

Jesse sort of like John Brown
Showing up to the struggle
just a little too early

Jesse my kind of hero
Unsung
Also-ran that made a difference
Number two that tried harder
Ahead of his time
Innovator
Pioneer
In the deep dark woods

of american politics

Those of us that can See
will always remember
Your role in the ascendancy
of the first black president

Jesse jumped on the grenade
Obama marched triumphant into the capitol
Obama doesn't make it
Without Jesse.

Dr. King

Some people call him Martin Luther King
Others MLK
to some, simply Martin
I like to call him Dr. King
I grew up in the 60s
and the way I saw it
the country was sick
and needed a doctor
and Dr. King was the guy for the job,
Dr. King—your Dad, your coach and your pastor
all rolled into one
calling on conscience
the higher angels of our nature,
whatever you want to call it
When he was around
the doctor was in
And it looked like the country
might have a chance.

Let Mystery Be!

Curveball, curveball
Now they gotta know it all

We used to be able to accept
the off-speed pitch;
we didn't care about the spin the ball had
when it left the pitcher's grip
content to wonder
whether it dipped or dropped out of the batter's reach
Or was it just an optical illusion?

But now
The TV analysis crew
with their impressive array of precision instruments
radar guns
and super-slow-motion cameras
minutely examine the spin of the ball
Counting each seam
Analyzing it frame by frame

micrometer by micrometer
then providing analysis of the analysis
Compiling, calibrating and cataloging
Into bar graphs and pie charts
Until they know every detail.
Stealing the awe from under our faces.

Curveball, curveball
Now they gotta know it all

Out beyond the ballparks
The dissections continue
Expeditions comb the hills
and plumb the lake depths,
seeking the solid evidence
that proves our monsters never existed
Spy satellites
map every square inch of the Earth
even the places we once dreamed of
as remote and wild
research vessels probe the ocean floors

nosing around in wrecks

to reveal a thousand details

better left to the deep

Curveball, curveball

Now they gotta know it all

Rip up the graphs and charts, I say!

Smash the measuring gadgets!

Shoot down the satellites!

Torpedo the research vessels!

Send em down to Davey Jones' locker!

And forbid anyone

from researching *why* they went down

Until they fade forever from our memory

Give us back our unknowns

Right now

Let mystery be!

Leave us free

To wonder again.

Dance

Each step
Each move
a natural expression of ourselves
Just the movement
and the rhythm
of our dance
our moves almost involuntary,
a reflex to the music.

Look at that one guy
slinking and slithering
like a snake across the dance floor
His dance
a coiling, wriggling advance toward the stage
like a sidewinder moving across the floor
in an S-shaped motion

Look at that young woman
Hips undulating
Calf muscles flexing
Colored lights reflecting off her dark hair
Her eyes closed,

Eyebrows raised as if in a trance

Check out that couple
Weaving in and out
of the pulsating rhythm
Each knowing the other's moves
Before they even make them
An awareness
Built from the knowing familiarity of lovers
their faces beaming with the
Joy of Movement

The techno rhythm trembles
The quickening thumps of bass and percussion
Fill the room to overflowing
Myriads of steps taken
Personalities displayed in movement
Blending together with the flashing lights
and quaking music
the whole floor in motion;
Fluid and natural
like a free-form
Expressionist painting.

Jerry-Rig

'Fixed'
instead of new
Slapped on
instead of a real fix
The Jerry Rig stands as a monument
to both man's laziness and his ingenuity

Duct tape, crazy glue and WD-40
Our holy trinity
Vice grips, pipe wrenches and sledge hammers
our favorite tools
We are the advocates of
spray painted car doors
and plastic bags as windows
our specialty—
things held together with baling wire
Or some nice solid pop rivets
Our jerry-rigged creations
Stagger like Frankensteins into a broken future

Such an american thing to do,
Just take two diametrically opposed elements

Slap them together
and hold them there flimsily, somehow
with some half-assed connecting device
and let er rip
It'll work, just watch.

As we use tools in a way
they were never meant to be used
Won't fit—make it fit
Bend it with pliers
Twist it with vice grips
Hit it with a hammer
Use a great big prybar.

Tape it
Glue it
Wire it
Tie it
Fuckit
Don't worry about it

Jerry rigs, quick fixes
our salvation, our savior
if they'd only just hold together.

NYC Rat

Aw man, look at that rat

here in NYC's Central Park

Sure is a big one

Thought he was a cat, or a small dog

Well-fed, too

Check out the fat, sagging stomach on him

How it drags down the stairs

of the park's stone steps

His long tail drags along, wriggling

His whiskers quiver

His teeth bared

Looks like a biter for sure!

I grew up in this city

Trained to kill rats on sight

But with this one,

I think I'm gonna jump in a taxi

and go far away.

Rat Rights

Back in the old days in New York
Old men told ya to kill rats on sight
Or they would take over the city
Like a lot of advice from old-timers
It was ignored
They stopped killing the rats
And now they have taken over the city.
They commute just like other New Yorkers
Running between the feet
of their fellow subway riders
They help themselves to unattended food
on the sidewalk cafe
They didn't do this stuff when I was a kid
Shit, now they probly got rat rights
The rat liberation movement
Preventing brutality to rats
Hey leave that greasy filthy
one of God's creatures alone
It's be nice to rat week
In fact we shouldn't even call em rats
Call em the pestilentially challenged
They should be on the endangered species list!

People try to pet rats nowadays
Be nice to em
Understand em
Hey, want a slice of pizza
Here, take mine
You want the room?
You got it
In fact take the whole city
We'll just move out.

In the Back of the Bus of Death

In the back of the bus of death
Dark silhouettes
of rough looking people
that got there via shotgun blast
or car wreck
or some other violent end

Better be on top of your game when you go
To the back of the bus of death
New arrivals take their seats
banged-up and bleeding

In the back of the bus of death,
Big dark silhouettes
the gleam of bald heads
Sweaty biceps
the tangle of tattoos
and shadows
of Fu-Manchus

The dark silhouettes of the dark souls
of the badass people

in the back of the bus of death.

And it's quiet, so quiet
All you can hear is the hum of the motor
and the tires singing on the pavement
like a dirge.

In the back of the bus of death,
Better be on top of your game
They ain't playin back there
Kill your sorry ass again
Send you down
to the death inside of death.

So sit down and be quiet
Cause you're takin that ride
all the way
To the End of the Line.

Ken's Kangaroo Court

Ken's Kangaroo Court

has found you guilty

You are my prisoner—and the penalty is death!

We don't care about that cruel and unusual shit, either

Death—by firing squad

And ya gotta smoke a cigarette, too

Unless you're a smoker—then ya can't have one

The firing squad smokes instead

First they fire up

Then they fire you up

That's the way we roll

in Ken's Kangaroo Court

It's can't or have to

Just to make sure it's cruel and unusual

And clearly unconstitutional

We do mean things

Like don't give a blindfold, unless ya don't want one

Then we make ya wear one

Other times we fake it

I give the ol' squad the order to fire

Then they don't fire

We do this six or seven times

We've had several heart attack deaths due to this

It's a shame

but it's worth it

That's the way it is

Can't or have to,

That's the way we roll

in Ken's Kangaroo Court.

Of Crazy Horse and Christ

The more I look at the lives
Of Crazy Horse and Christ
The more I think they're very much alike
Look at the similarities:

Both didn't own anything
Both went out into the wilderness
to have visions
Both claimed to have supernatural powers
Crazy Horse said he was bulletproof
Christ claimed he was the son of God
Both were killed by their own people,
The Romans washed their hands of Christ
The US Army washed its hands of Crazy Horse

Yes, you could say Christ didn't
Steal horses or kill people
That is a big difference,
but largely a cultural one,

a matter of time and place.

Still, there are many more similarities

than differences

Any way one looks at it

a case can be made

That Crazy Horse and Christ

Were much alike.

Three Stooges vs. PC

PC people are appalled by the Three Stooges

and all their verbal and physical abuse

What would happen if they could change all that?

Well, it would be straight to sensitivity training for Moe

His words are hurtful

Look at all that negative reinforcement

he dumps on his pals

He could use some anger management class

In fact, all three of these guys could

Larry is sporting some problems too

He enables Moe

and when he beats on Curly

That's solid evidence of displaced aggression

Textbook passive aggressive behavior

Our boy needs therapy and plenty of it

It's hard to tell what's wrong with Curly

He's definitely got ADD

with a little OCD thrown in

He's rarely rational, if ever

what a mess

And how about that Shemp?

and the way he behaves around women

Can't even talk to em,

Just makes funny noises

and slaps himself in the back of the head

as if he's re-setting himself

Such incredible passivity toward women

can only lead to terrible aggression in the future

Get him some help before it's too late

Lets face it

This whole bunch needs a lot of work.

The McDali Lama

Never thought I'd see it
But it happened
the old Dalai Lama died
after many years
And what to do about replacing him?
They couldn't go back to find
the Tibetan baby boy
Reincarnated with the Dalai Lama's spirit
Tibet is not a country anymore
So what could they do
The US government still wanted to have one
the CIA always liked the guy
So it was decided
to find another Dalai Lama, right here in America
McDonald's offered to sponsor the search
But only if they could include their brand name
and that my friends
is how they came up with
the McDali Lama.

Fuckin Cosell

Fuckin Cosell

That's what we'd always say

Shaking our heads

As he used all these big words

in his nasal voice

Acting all superior again

Thought he was God's intellectual gift to the world

Another guy who thought he was smarter than he was

But we liked him anyway

I can still hear him saying, this is Howard Cosell,

Speaking of Sports on the radio….

I remember him on TV too

in his yellow ABC jacket

on Wide World of Sports

A man with puffy eyes

a nose even bigger than his ego

and obvious, off-brown toupee

But it was the voice that got to us

that high, nasal whine

Always using big words

Too big a words

Like when something didn't happen

Cosell would say, "that did not eventuate".

or if something was unlikely,

he'd say, "it's not reasonably probable"

Or when describing demolition derby

on Wide World of Sports

He called it the "organized destruction of cars"

Fuckin Cosell

That's what we'd say

Then we'd shake our heads

Pompous ass

but still, a lovable one

Friendly contempt

Good natured scorn

We acted like we hated him,

but we loved him deep-down.

We had sort of a backhand respect for him, too
at the end of the day, he knew his shit
Especially about boxing.
He was the first to call Muhammed Ali
Muhammed Ali when he changed his name
Everybody knew that.
And, he didn't need us to humble him
Real life took care of that

I saw him once
attempting to 'dash' out of Madison Square Garden
to his limousine
He could hardly make it
A much older man than we saw on TV
little kids were imitating him
when he couldn't open the door
little black kids holding imaginary microphones
up to their mouths and saying
'There's Howard Cosell trying but failing
to open his limousine door.'
It was another fucked up New York moment

Funny, if it wasn't you

I try to forget about it

I prefer to remember Howard

in all his past splendor.

I can still hear him saying,

this is Howard Cosell, Speaking of Sports

in the radio shows of my memory

I can still see him

on Monday Night Football, in all his glory

with Frank Gifford and Don Meredith

Brash and bragging

Cocooning himself with big words

Fuckin Cosell

that's what we'd always say….

Cure

Oh you gotta run
when they try to cure you, boy
Run away fast and far
Cause when they get busy curing
You've got to put lots of ground
Between you and them.

When they cure you
they put you in a truck
I seen it
They came and took away my buddy from the park
and all he was doing was living under a spruce tree
and drinkin a few beers on a bench
Then they came with that big white truck
and took him away
I asked em why
they said he was sick,
they were gonna cure him.

I hate to think of him in there
I've heard what they do to you
with their psychologists

and their counselors
and their classes
that teach you how to be a good boy
and their therapy, therapy, therapy

like well-meaning zombies
with their eyes blind
and their hands grabbing
They turn your head around
and upside down
Smiling faces say let us help you
faces attached to people with weird ideas
about what helpful and harmful are
Just ask the people overseas
that they've 'helped'
as they drag their dead from burning rubble
courtesy of these helpful people
who would kill to cure
who would drop bombs to protect freedom
Hell no, I wouldn't let them cure me
Run boy, like the hammers of hell
when they try to cure you
You better run boy
Run!

HMO Poem

Sure doesn't look like a place of healing
with all that steel and glass.
Looks more like a corporate headquarters building
Full of people who want to take your money
and it doesn't take long for you to be proved right.
The first thing you do is pay
Right as you walk in
Payment demanded by bored clerks
From behind big sterile counters
Security just down the hall
in case you want to raise hell about it

Guess they really don't care how it looks
$ their main objective
Everything else comes in a distant second
including patient care
But don't tell them that
They'll get all righteous and indignant
How can you say that?
Patient care is our utmost priority
as they count the money in the till

They try to hide it
But it keeps breaking through
Everything smells of this mercenary, mercantile attitude
Every treatment or drug tracked down
to the last fraction of a penny
Our health care system
Really just a microcosm
of our whole economic system
Big profits for the few
Big bills for the many
Everybody's gonna get sick one day
and don't they know it
and take full advantage of it
Somebody's making a whole lot of money
While a lot of us have substandard coverage
Or none at all

When you finally walk out the door
You look back at the
corporate headquarters-type building
Sure doesn't look like a place of healing
You don't feel cured
Neither does your wallet.

Ahead of the Storms

Sometimes

when me and my old travelling buddies

were cruising the country

going wherever we wanted

for a little while

We'd see storms on the TV radar

coming in from the west

So we'd hop in our cars and head east

Ahead of the storms

Just....leaving them behind

Sometimes seeing the clouds

build up in our rearview mirrors before we left

Picturing the storms streaming east

on a weathercaster's map

and us just ahead of them

Just ahead of the storms

and the feeling it gave, of a close call

or wriggling off the hook

Lucky escapees

Young, free and unattached

Just ahead of the storms.

To My Great Grandmother

Just a distant, faded memory now
Dead for more than thirty years;
Even when alive, just seen on holidays,
Someone that didn't say much
that didn't say anything.
Just sat at the far end of the couch
Away.

She looked ancient,
even back then
Thin wisps of white hair
barely covering the scalp
almost bald
Had no teeth,
made no attempt to put them in
Giving the face that concave look
like a peanut
Crinkled sockets cradling clouded eyes
Cheeks hollowed, nose and chin sagging

The full weight of ninety-plus years of gravity
Showing on the face.

I never knew if she heard me or not;
I remember my Grandmother, her daughter
talking real loud right in front of her face
It would register, sort of
I don't think I ever heard her formulate
a word back to us
Just made these little whimpers;
upbeat at the end if she was happy
downbeat at the end if she wasn't

But I remember how she came back to us
From wherever it was that she stayed
Whenever my Grandma asked if she wanted
to hold my little cousin when she was a baby
the maternal instinct awakening
after being dormant for so long
She knew just how to hold the baby
And the baby knew she was in good hands, too

Grew quiet right away.
Great-Grandma peering down
Making funny faces at the baby
Snuggling with her
Making little cooing noises
It was like she came back to life
Just for that time.

I don't remember much else about her
except how my Grandmother
used to always encourage my two brothers and I
Write your great-grandma at the Home
When she gets letters from you guys
It makes her so happy
She carries them around
like they're worth a million dollars.

Hurdler

Oh look at the hurdler
As he slowly and painfully
peels off his sweat pants,
His poor legs
displaying the damage
of a season's worth
of 110 meter high hurdle races
Look at all those bumps and bruises
He's black
He's blue
He's purple, green and yellow
The legs telling how tough
The season has been
A season of hurdles snapping back
and chiseling into shins
A season of getting bumped and spiked
A season of tripping, staggering
and one or two falls
Those legs tell the story
of hurdle hitting man
Man hitting man
Man hitting the track

and getting abrased and contused

The legs tell the story
of a hard season
the bumps and bruises
like harpoons sticking out of Moby Dick.

Relay System

Must have been tough
Being a large mammal
In the prehistoric era
Being hunted by us
Something on two legs
That works together
that can chase you forever
Something much more telepathic than today
And the worst thing of all—
Something that had a relay system
That's what really killed ya
If you were prey in the day
Full, fresh packs of pursuers
One after another
You guys chase em to us
then we'll chase em
to those guys, etc, etc.
An animal can't out-think or outrun that
Relay system a death sentence for the hunted
No wonder so many of them went extinct.
Relay system so embedded in our memory;
Ancient craft, vital skill

Leading to successful hunts
and meat.

Perhaps this is why
Relay races are still popular to this day.
The Penn Relays, the NCAAs, the Olympics
There are even massive relay races
that cover hundreds of miles
much like the hunts of our ancient ancestors
Relay system
Burned like a brand into our brain
Memories of ancient hunts
Being kept alive.

Crazy

Know what it's like?

It's like you were driving along

free and easy

But somehow you ended up in the back seat

Strapped into the baby chair

And some warped, whacked guy

Who looks just like you--

Scared, sweaty, eyes real big

Driving like a maniac

making the worst moves possible

almost hitting other cars and pedestrians

and you just sit there and watch him

and can't do a thing

about

it.

No Shoelaces

Sure wish they'd give my shoelaces back

Here in the Mental Health Center

When you say you're suicidal

they take ya kinda serious

No belts or shoelaces

Push button showers with no heads

Shatterproof windows that can't be opened

Spoons only, no forks or knives

I understand

Their job is to keep us alive and everything

But still

It's a drag looking down at my laceless sneakers

Come on guys

It's a constant reminder

Couldn't I please just have them back?

How about just one set?

I'll be a good boy, I always tell them

But I can tell

They're not gonna budge on this

Guess I'll have to learn to live with it

But I tell ya what

When I finally do get my shoelaces back

I'm gonna lace up my sneakers

and walk away from here so fast

That I won't even need a car.

Empath

Some say that peoples' first reaction

Is to argue or fight

I don't agree

Especially after working as a canvasser

Door to door

I think people's first reaction is to help

That's how we got out of the cave, isn't it?

Empathy

that ability to put yourself in the other guy's place

Hey—that would suck if it happened to me

think I'll help out.

This leading to other abilities

Like getting a message across

sharing new ideas

and making them happen

it wasn't every man for himself

when we got out of the cave

it was hands reaching out

Everybody helping everybody

Sharing information,

not hiding it away

Pooling resources then,

not hoarding them

It was helping hands

That got us out of the cave

Not a profit motive.

What the hell happened?

Work that Sign, Bro

Up and down the sidewalk
He marches along
at a brisk pace
Holding up a sign that says
Support the Troops
I was against both wars myself
I'm anti-war, I think
well, I draw the line at bar fights.
At any rate, I'm fascinated by this guy
no matter what his sign says
He shows up every day
rain or shine
His tangled beard and his tousled hair
His taped-together glasses
in a tee shirt, shorts and sneakers
He parades back and forth incessantly
Why does he do it?
What drives this man?
I've never seen him take any money
The cars honk to show their support
guess that's good enough for him.
He replies to the beep-applause

with a dead-serious thumbs-up
and goes back to grimly pacing
He's not a pan-handler
Just marches with a sign
I don't know why.

Maybe he's like me
Needs something to do
to stay out of trouble
Maybe he just views it as his job
Without it he'd be bored
and idle
He might even go crazy!

So he reports to this,
His work-station, his post
Tramping back and forth
like he means business
all day long with his big sign
That he carries like a cross
Rain or shine
at a near-frantic pace
Like his life depended on it,
like he'd die if he stopped.

Old Man Role Models

The world better not

let me live to be an old man

I'm gonna be the wildest old man there ever was

I have excellent role models to go by

Observed in the Revlon Cosmetic factory

in the bathroom of the Creams and Lotions department

on graveyard shift at 5:00 in the morning

That's when they briefly shut down assembly lines

to work on the machines, get them ready for Day Shift

Some of us snuck away

on unofficial break to smoke in the bathroom

in the good old days when you could do that

These old men would come in

pushing and shoving

like little kids, only old

Unshaven, with messed up hair

Stains on the shirts of their lifer uniforms

They didn't give a fuck what they looked like

These men with white heads that shook with mirth

Laughing and wheezing at the same time

Some of them doing little dances

and jumping around

as much as an old man can jump

They smoked non-filters in that bathroom

of creams and lotions at 5:00 AM

What wild old guys

They'd come back from the weekend

with black eyes

and bruised knuckles

Hey—where's what's his name

Oh, arrested was he?

They kicked ass while they were on the clock, too

Wiry old silver-backed monkeys

That scrambled up and down assembly lines

Keeping the assemblers supplied with components

What they'd lost in brawn, they made up in brains

They could just look at an assembly line

and tell how fast it was gonna run

how quickly it would run out of something, and where
They finished strong, too
Keeping way ahead of the work all the way to the end.

And after the shift
They went straight to the bar across the street
Just like the young guys
got hammered
went home and crashed
While it was still daylight
Then woke up in the evening
And did it all again

Yeah, the world better not
let me live to be an old man
because I have excellent
Old man role models.

Just Say Yeah

There's two ways to deal with
Things you don't want to do in this life
Things you don't agree with but get forced to do
One way is to fight it head on
Although this is the more principled stand
It can get long, drawn-out
Might take a lot of time
and maybe even blood.

But there is another way to deal with this problem
Just say yeah
Yeah   Yeah
    Yeah   Yeah
Then go do whatever ya want.

Yep, yeah has been a good tool over the years
it's served me well, got me through a lot of opposition
Yeah   Yeah
    Yeah   Yeah
Been sayin it for years
ever since kindergarten

Still using it today
Yeah, mixed with the occasional I hear ya
an incidental nod here and there
Use it liberally on teachers, bosses
cops and judges
Yeah   Yeah
   Yeah   Yeah

Good for domestic use, too
in the home, on your spouse
Just add honey
Yeah honey, yeah honey
you don't even have to be married
It's not a sin to use pre-marital yeahs.

Yeah works great at work
Hey, we need you to have this done today
by yourself, yeah, yeah, yeah
Hey we need people to work late, yeah, yeah, yeah
Hey, go make the coffee again, yeah, yeah, yeah

Sometimes people say yeah to you
I hate that
I mean, you're trying to tell the guy something important

and he's going
Yeah		Yeah
　　Yeah			Yeah
and ya know what the guy is doing
Cause you do it to the other guys!

Who did I use yeah on lately?
It was someone really obnoxious and pushy
Richly deserving of the yeah treatment
forget who it was now but anyway
Yeah has always worked well for me, son
I always keep it in my social skills toolbox
Yeah		Yeah
　　Yeah			Yeah

Then I go do whatever I want.

Bad Road Food

Bitter coffee that's been sitting for hours

Stale donuts

Hamburgers burned through and through

Twice-fried french fries

Overly greasy chicken

Overly greasy everything

All of it, all of it

to strengthen and fortify us

For the tough road conditions ahead

Giving us the ferocious attitude we need

to jump behind the wheel again

and knock off a few hundred more miles

The bad coffee especially helpful

to keep our eyes wide open and unblinking

as white line after white line

pass us by on the road

The car speeding toward tiny lights

on a dark horizon

The vastness of the country

truly impressing itself upon us

The incredible distances dwarf us

as we seem to crawl across an endless landscape

The longer states feeling like whole countries

Time seems to slow down

Then stand still entirely

The radio doesn't pick up any stations anymore

just the sound of whining tires fill the void

We seem ready to fly right up

into the star-sparkled sky

But ragged clouds hold us back

and we pass by the lights

of houses where people remain stationary

Maybe never straying from that spot

for their entire lives

Not us--always moving, moving

Always more and more road

rushing toward the windshield

Our eyelids get heavy

and our asses hurt

The tough conditions strengthening us

the physical strain of the drive

Plus the bad road food

Equals successful journey.

A Bird's Life

Ever notice how many people
say they'd like to come back as a bird
Free as a bird,
that's what people say
But how free are they, really?
How great is a bird's life, anyway?
They always have to watch out
for bigger, more predatory birds
and they have to chase smaller birds or bugs
in order to eat.
Hunters try to shoot them down,
rotten kids with BB guns, too.
There are other hazards
Like cars
and electrical wires
and glass—that glass is a real bitch

Basically, you have to fly
All the time
The sky a vast prairie
that must be tread with wings

The clouds white mountains
that must be climbed
What if you're tired that day?

And you have to fly down South
for the winter
I don't like it much down South, y'all

So it turns out that free as a bird
is another thing that ain't true
Bird chained to sky
As man is chained to ownership

A bird's life has its problems, too
It's no picnic
Glad I'm a man.

21st Century Elves

The 21st century is starting on a bad note

if you ask me

There's all these wars and terrorism

Such an impersonal century, too

Nobody cares

Half the people out there

don't do their jobs

It's even spread to the elves

who used to be very dependable workers

Literally working miracles overnight

Not anymore, boy

21st century elves leave you their work now

They don't do nothin—not even the dishes

21st century elves loiter all night on your front porch

like teenagers at a 7-11

21st century elves got attitude, too

They sneer and make a face

when you ask em to do something

21st century elves say bad things about ya

You can hear them whispering

just outside the bathroom door.

21st century elves trash your house

when you go on vacation

They smoke stinky elf weed

and leave the roaches laying on the floor

21st century elves are lazy as hell

worthless and weak

stubborn and stupid

21st century elves take your last beer.

Bottles Don't Last

Bottles don't last long around here

Hobbled, they stagger back

Wounded, they retreat

The ones that stick around

Become dead soldiers fast.

Bottles don't last long around here

Throw the cap away, that's what we say

No such thing as a liquor cabinet

in this here house

Keepin half-full bottles

behind closed doors

Man, what for?

Some people

Actually lock their liquor cabinet

with a key

Can you believe that?

What if you get so drunk

Ya lose it?

What then?

Bottles don't last long around here

Ya feel sorry for em

Honest ta God

The way they just keep comin

and keep gettin knocked over

Ya'd think they'd wise up sooner or later.

Bottles don't last long around here

We just throw em down

and kick em outta the way

They lay all over

Tipped on their sides

They roll into corners

or wedge themselves under couches and chairs

Who knows where they end up

who cares either.

Bottles don't last long around here

Some of em act big and tough, too

Quarts, even half gallons

Towering high

As we rest our heads on the table

We get up, take the standing 8 count

and say, oh yeah, bring it

And before ya know it

They're a dead soldier too

Up they come, down they go

The bigger they come,

the harder they fall

Bottles don't last long around here.

One More Won't Hurt

Went to a funeral today

Then came straight back to the bar

with the guys

To have another drink

One more won't hurt.

It was Charlie Goodwin today

Poor Charlie

he was one of the guys, too.

We raised a toast to our old buddy.

This keeps on happening

People we've been drinking with for years

Suddenly get sick and die

Then we go to the funeral

and march straight back to the bar and drink

till another one of us goes

We keep doing this over and over

like we're on a conveyor belt

That ends at the cemetery

It's cradle to bar to grave for us.

Once in a while, we look in the mirror behind the bar

and get a glimpse of what we really look like

A few of us might even get a fleeting thought

Of doing something about it

But we can never fully take that step

the buzz overrules everything

So we order another round

What the hell

One more won't hurt.

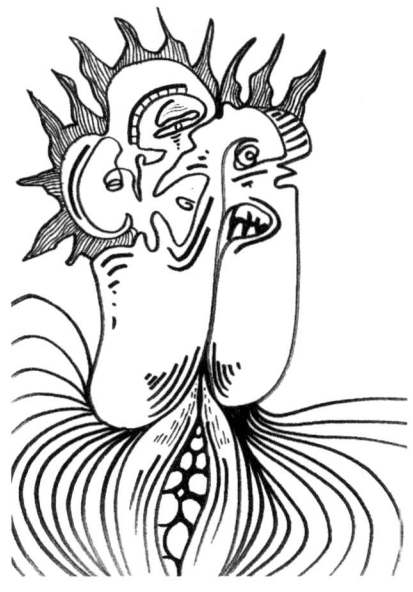

My Uncle and the Full Moon

Earth and moon

sisters in Space

Full moon tugging on the Earth

moving whole oceans

Allegedly pulling on us too

the human body is mostly water

Full moon high tide in the brain…..

My uncle the New York cop believed in its power

He said as a policeman on the job

He'd seen all kinds of people go crazy from it

He told so many stories

of full-moon influenced bad behavior

I told my grandmother, his mother, about this

She said, that's because it works on him.

And I think she was right

I remember several times

My uncle looking up at the full moon

Ooh, look at that, he'd say

followed by a big grin

and a mysterious chuckle

and the way he looked

Psyched—like he couldn't wait

to hit the streets

and collide with other NYC people

Crazed by the full moon

God only knows

What they got up to out there.

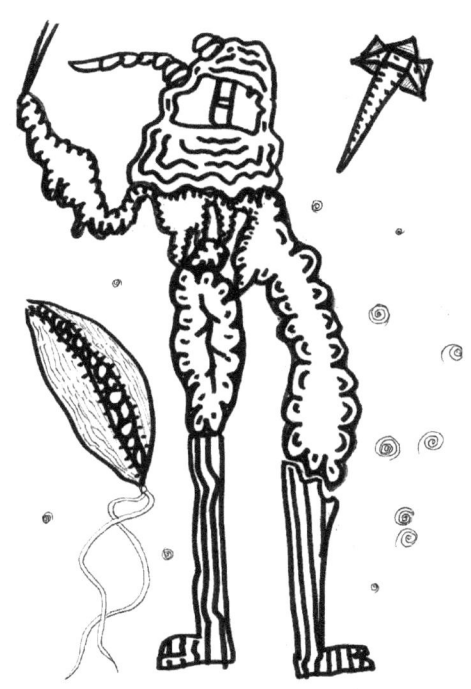

Godspot

There it is

a small square

in the corner of my ceiling

A special spot I look up to

and say thank you up there

whenever something cool happens

whenever I get in a close one

and get out of it

whenever appropriate

Call it my Godspot.

I look up and thank my Godspot

When good guys win over bad

when reason overrules anger

whenever empathy melts the frost.

I look up and thank my Godspot

for my wife

for the food

for the roof

I look up and thank my Godspot

for the luck

the life

the love

the writing

and the Dreaming.

I look up and thank my Godspot

and give thanks for everything

every day

Almost.

Them and Their Tries

Tried to barge in and take over

Tried to be a big obstacle

Tried to call the shots in my game

Them and their tries.

Tried to make me someone I wasn't

Tried to get in the way of my Dreams

Tried to change my mind

and stifle my soul

Tried to scare me

With foreign boogeymen

Tried to spin my head around

and upside down

with their cable TV experts

Tried to get me to sign up

for one of their wars

Them and their tries.

Tried to tell me there'd be big trouble
if I walked out on their Class
Told me I'd die, if I didn't do it their way.

Tried to tell me I had a tough road ahead,
I better quit and get a full time job
Tried to stop me
from writing these poems to you.

Them and their tries.

Tried to tell me
        how to look
        what to think
        who to hang out with
        where to go
        and when

Them and their tries.

Flash Fiction

Doesn't Believe in Angels

"And then he says he doesn't believe in angels! That's what kills me!" The angel hunches over the bar, complains to the bartender here at the Cloud Nine Lounge, a bar frequented by off-duty angels. It's an after-work bar; the angels come here to commiserate about their human wards. All their wings are hung up neatly on hooks on the wall. Billowy clouds fill the big front window opposite the bar.

The angel sits sprawled at the bar. He looks haggard, his eyes are bloodshot and half-open, his hair is all messed up. "You should see all the sh—," he winces, "I mean the *stuff* I've gotten this guy out of."

The bartender rolls his eyes and pours him another shot, gets him another beer. He's an older angel, big bags under his eyes, deep lines in the face. A heaven-weary angel. He looks on as the angel on the other side of the bar continues his rant.

"This guy would be screwed a hundred times over if it wasn't for me." He shakes his head. "So many close ones. There was that time when he was a kid, his friends bet him he couldn't bury the speedometer, you know, get it to go 120 down a country road. I tried to tell him not to do it, that there might be sharp curves ahead. But does he listen? Hell, no!"

"Then that other time, that woman's comin onto him, kickin her legs, and shakin her ass. He's all hot and bothered. Tell him no, don't do it, you know you're married. I even told him to look at the ring, look at the ring on your finger. So what does he do? He goes for it anyway!" Again he shakes his head, stares down at the floor. "You shoulda seen how long it took me to clean up that mess."

The senior, heaven-weary angel barkeep looks at him, nods once or twice.

"And it's not just that," the whiney angel continues. "He drinks like crazy!"

Some of the other angels in the room

stop talking now and look over at him.

"Aw right, I know, I drink too. But with this guy it's wretched excess. I mean he takes a bath in the sh—, I mean the stuff. It's more than that, even. Sometimes he tries to get into fights with other dudes, he gets in trouble with the cops, too. I tell ya, he's a handful," he rubs his hand over his face, "a real handful."

The bartender folds his arms over his chest. The other angels look at each other.

"But that's not the worst of it." The guardian angel continues whining. "There's other things, too. I mean besides the physical threats or practical everyday matters. It's a *soul* we're talking about here, a man's soul." He clutches his fist in front of his chest. "A man's *soul*!"

By now the bartender-angel has moved to the other end of the bar. The other angels roll their eyes, start to murmur.

"I mean, sometimes I have to fight like

hell, er excuse me, I have to really struggle hard, just to keep the guy on an even keel. I mean the guy's a whacko. Sometimes he gets so bitter and so angry, his heart just fills up with hatred, and I swear, sometimes I think I'll never get him out of it. Other times he's dark. So dark. He just thinks everything is sad and hopeless, he doesn't believe in anything anymore. He just gives up on it all. Withdraws from everything. Gets to the point where I seriously wonder if he'll off himself and put me out of a job! Ah, it's such a weight looking after a man's soul!"

"We know!" One angel shouts.

"We do that too, remember?" Another one chimes in.

The whiney angel seems not to hear them. "And the worst thing, the worst thing of all," he holds up a drunken finger. "Is that he says he doesn't believe in angels. That what kills me the worst of all. I mean I do all these favors for him, steer him out of all this trouble, save him from certain doom all the time…And then he says he doesn't believe in angels." He throws his hands up and slumps on the stool. "Doesn't believe in angels!"

"Ah, dry up buddy!" One angel shouts. "You're not the only one with a hard case!"

"What hard case? Mine's a lawyer—for an HMO!"

"Mine's a politician—from New Jersey!"

"Mine's a reality show producer—from hollywood!"

"Ugh!" All the angels groan together.

"Well, he could at least acknowledge me!" says the whiner angel.

"Ah, boo-hoo!"

"Yeah, this is heaven, pal. Count yer blessings."

Come to the Realization

Some people have a hard time facing facts. About anything unpleasant. They just turn away and hope it will evaporate. They can't 'come to the realization'. Whenever I see a situation like this, that phrase comes to mind. The first time I heard it was in county jail. They booked me, got my basic information, then shoved me into the holding cell.

All the other prisoners looked at me. This is the moment of truth, when they first put you in there. The other prisoners all check you out. "Are you predator? Or prey?" is the inferred question. I answered 'predator' with my eyes. After all, I was in for assault. Some asshole was being as loud as he could on his cell phone. I told him to shut up. He said fuck you. So here I was. True, I started swinging first. It was minor shit, case ended up getting dismissed.

Anyway, for now here I was in the holding tank. I checked out the other prisoners. Nobody looked that tough, luckily. And nobody fucked with me. Yet. I didn't see the other dude I was fighting with, either. Hmm.

More and more prisoners started to arrive. There was a wave that came in right after 2:00 AM. Tensions rose as less and less bench space was available. Some near-fights occurred, with people getting in each others' face. But they all ended the same way, with one guy backing out grudgingly, grumbling, and finding a space somewhere else.

A guy came in after me answered 'Prey' to the inferred question. He looked scared, he had the big eyes. I saw another prisoner scope out the guy, then nudge his partner in the ribs, look at him. Looked like possible trouble ahead.

One guy came in with his chest stuck out. He had greasy curly hair. He looked at all the other guys firmly and evenly, then sat down at the first spot he saw. Other guys moved. He definitely wasn't prey.

The time slowly passed. The door opened

and a guard shoved two more guys into the tank with us.

"When's the pizza get here?" The bigger guy chuckled at us and grinned. He seemed like an amiable enough dude. Good thing, looked like he weighed about 250 and had a shaved head.

"Damn, man." His smaller friend circled his hand around and his wrist and rubbed it. "Those cuffs were on so tight. My hands are numb, mothafucker." You could tell this guy didn't give a fuck what he said to anyone. In fact, one quick look at this pair, and you could see it in a flash. The little guy was the mouth and the big guy was the muscle he called on. The big guy had a bunch of lumps on his head that seemed to bear out the theory.

"How you gents doing?" he flashed another grin. After a while, me and them asked each other the traditional question. "What are you in for?" I told them my tale.

"Fighting! Us too!" the big guy said.

"Yeah," the little guy added excitedly. "We got kicked out of the bar, then we started fightin the bouncers outside. Fuckin assholes. Then the cops came, and we just started fightin them!" He laughed uproariously.

The big guy confirmed the story with another big grin. He rubbed the lumps on his head.

"Shit man," the little guy said. "Them fuckin handcuffs hurt, nigger!"

Great, I thought, now he's gonna start a racial confrontation in here. I looked at the black dudes in the tank with us. They didn't say anything. Looked like they were playin it cool. They knew beatin on some white punks wouldn't help them get out of here any sooner.

The two guys sat down in the corner. It was quiet for a while. The holding tank absorbed its prisoners.

Later on, I started pacing the cell and passed by these two. "Fuck man," the little guy said. "I guess we should figure out how to get outta here."

"We'll have to call your old man for starters."

"Oh shit," the little guy said. "It's the weekend, ain't it?"

"Memorial Day weekend," the big guy chuckled.

"Aagh!" The little guy held his head in his hands. "That means we're gonna be in here…. for three days?!"

"Dude, come to the realization."

The little guy let out a prolonged groan.

Ever since, any time I am in a similar situation, I hear the words, come to the realization, and my mind snaps back to this jailhouse memory.

Overtime in Omaha

My wife and I had been sitting in the Greyhound station in Omaha, Nebraska for four hours, with nothing to do and nowhere to go. At last all the passengers and us boarded. We were about to hit the road. Suddenly an old woman in one of the front seats turned and punched the guy next to her right in the face. She did it a couple of times. We could hear her connecting, that hollow sound of a fist hitting a half-open mouth.

"You bastard!" she yelled. "You sexually harassed me!"

"You're crazy!" the guy next to her said. But he looked the part. A chubby middle-aged guy with glasses and a big mustache like guys in 1970s porn movies have. Isn't it always guys who look like that?

The bus driver threw it into park. Everybody jerked forward. The driver, a tall black man, made his way down the aisle. "What the hell's going on back heah?"

"He sexually harassed me!"

"No I didn't!"

The woman started yelling some more. She had a big hawk nose, made her whole face look like a bird's.

The driver stopped her with a braking motion of the hands. "But ma'am, you hit this guy."

"No I didn't."

"Yes you did. I saw y'all in the rearview mirror."

"Well, he deserved it. He grabbed my…."

"Aw right, aw right ma'am." The driver looked at her and the guy with a quick, assessing look. He blew out a deep breath. "I'm gonna hafta ask both of you to get off the bus."

"Why me?" the alleged harasser said.

"I can't," the old woman said. "I'm sick. My heart," she clutched at her chest. "I have to get to Denver and see my doctor."

"Oh Jesus," I said to my wife. The bus fell quiet.

The driver made an awkward attempt to grab one of the old woman's arms.

"Don't touch me! I'll sue Greyhound!"

The driver let out another deep breath, and rolled his eyes. He shrugged, then skulked to the front of the bus. "Ladies and gentlemen, his voice crackled over the intercom. "There will be a short delay."

The whole bus groaned at once. The driver put the bus in gear, drove around the block and pulled right back into the station. We all groaned again. It was back to the waiting room for us.

And what a waiting room. Dirty floors, garbage cans overflowing. It was too small for the amount of people we had. A lot of us ended up standing. Including me. It was hot and stuffy. It smelled like a room that too many people were stuffed in to wait.

Just standing around was a drag. There was no bar in this station, and no smoking either.

We thought to go outside, but the neighborhood didn't look too cool. It looked like a lot of Midwest cities looked in the late 20th century, the wreckage of an old downtown area. Abandoned buildings, boarded up storefronts, crackhouses, garbage blowing down streets hardly inhabited by anyone.

Nothing to do out there. And nothing to do in here either. My wife finally found a seat, me and her shared it.

Sitting/standing there for hours, bored out of our minds, again. The waiting room seemed even smaller, hotter and stuffier. Every minute felt like a month. I had visions of never getting out. Stuck here forever, like one of those nightmares when you're running like hell, but keep ending up at the same place.

After what seemed like centuries, a voice finally squawked over the intercom. "Bus number 13 headed to Denver is now boarding."

Sighs of relief and Thank Gods filled the air. We re-boarded. I looked for the old woman and the alleged harasser. New passengers filled their seats. Hmmm.

The bus finally lumbered out of the station, rolled out of downtown and toward Interstate 80 West. We were on our way at last.

The Old Riots

Today's riots inevitably bring back memories of the old ones, which occurred in the middle and late 1960s. I think they were worse than those of today. Well, all riots suck, anytime, anywhere. Still, a lot more people were getting hurt and killed. The cops were shooting at people and people were shooting back. At least that's what the cops said. Those riots were a lot more violent, and there were more of them. There was strife in every city at once, not just a few. And it went on and on, for days and weeks.

Also, the president at the time, Lyndon Johnson, decided it would be a good idea to send national guard troops to the cities. I'll never forget that. To me, he took the riots personally. He had just signed the Civil Rights Act in 1965. I guess it was a case of too little too late. Cause the riots started in 1967. Looked to me like Johnson got pissed because of this. "What—I just signed that bill, and now they're rioting? Fuckit, I'll send the troops in." Just like he did in Vietnam. No wonder the guy was a one-termer. He was even worse than the Bushes as president. And he was a Democrat!

I'll never forget that bastard sending troops into the cities. Now you had scared suburban white kids in the jeeps with fifty caliber machine guns, going into a ghetto environment they knew nothing about. People who lit a cigarette in the window got shot to pieces with machine gun fire.

We were white and lived in the suburbs, so the riots only touched us peripherally. At first, it was just something on TV. Then one day my Dad and I drove over a bridge that passed over the New Jersey Turnpike. Below us, jeeps and armored personnel carriers full of helmeted troops slowly headed north to Newark.

"Hey Dad, what's with the army going up to Newark?"

He just shrugged and muttered something about 'the coons'.

It's too bad. My Dad was an educated man. He should have known better, based on in-the-field experience. I guess conditioning had something to do with it. He grew up in New York in the 1940s and 50s. There wasn't a whole lot of integration going on. Every racial group feared, mistrusted and stayed away from the other. Least that's what my father and grandparents said.....Anyway, that brief comment was all I could get out of my Dad on the subject. A lot of peoples' Dads were like that back then. That's part of the reason there were riots.

My mother wouldn't talk about it either. Or any of my friends' parents. For me, that was the worst part of it. I mean, you're watchin cities burn and cops shooting at people on the TV news, and no adults will tell ya what the hell's going on.

Us kids were left to talk about it amongst ourselves. And we didn't get very far. I remember my friend Brian Wienstein talking about the riots coming to our town. There we were in the middle of a belt of white-bread suburbs, and we're worried about 'them' coming 'here'.

I said so what, if they come, we can just take off into the woods. I was talking about the mile-deep woods that began at the dead end down the street. That was my answer for everything back then. And it kinda still is.

My buddy Brian wasn't buying it. "They'll just come through the woods after us, or in through the other side."

"Then we'll just take the back roads out of here, out by Crazy Joe's farm."

Brian shook his head. "Ya can't go there, either. They come from every direction."

That always stuck in my mind. They come from every direction. Like they were omniscient, omnipresent. Like God. Tttt. Well, that's how white kids in the suburbs were thinking at that time.

So that's the way it went for us, seeing cities burn, people fighting in the street, hearing of atrocity and murder. And to top it off, surrounded by adults that didn't want to talk about it.

It finally took an old white woman from the

south, my great aunt, to straighten me out on the whole thing. She even called herself Dixie.

"Hey Dixie, what's going on? Why is everybody so mad?"

"What, your folks didn't talk to you about this?"

I shook my head no.

She shook her head too.

"Well, she began slowly. "They—black people—" she bit her lip, "they were our slaves."

"Huh?"

"Our slaves. We went over there and grabbed em from Africa. Brought em over here."

"Whoa!"

"Yeah. That's why they're so mad. Well, one of the reasons."

I was so young, I just said. "Well, why don't they just send em back?"

My great-aunt started laughing. "A lot of people would like to do that. But it's not that simple."

"How come?"

"Well, they've been here for generations... years and years, just like us. They've been here longer than anyone. Well, except the Indians...." She looked at me. "You don't understand, do you? Well, it's a complicated issue. There's more to it. They can't get good jobs. They're poor. They live in run-down houses, in bad parts of every city."

"Why?"

"I don't know." She shrugged. "It just kind of...got going that way, and no one knows how to stop it. Well, the government is trying to stop it, but then there's people who want it to stay that way, there's all this pushin and shovin, and I guess that's why people are so mad. Oh, I don't know. It's a mess." She threw her hands up. "You'll understand it all better when you get older." That's how she wound up the conversation. Well, at least she tried to explain it, which is more that I can say for my parents....

Those were wild times. Cities burning. Cops and people shooting it out in the street. I'm sure glad I wasn't in the middle of it. Still, just knowing it was happening was a cause of shame for every American, including me. And it was really hard trying to find out anything about it, with practically no adults wanting to talk about it at all.

Playing in the DDT

My mother told us not to play in the DDT. But my brother and me wouldn't listen. This was in a simpler time, when DDT was legal. And it was in a swampy place, New Jersey, where a lot of mosquitoes congregate. So a few times every summer a truck would ride through our neighborhood, spraying gigantic white clouds of DDT to kill off the little pests. And then all the kids in the neighborhood would get on their bicycles and follow the truck like it was a pied piper, laughing and riding into the big white billows.

"You kids stay away from that truck," my mother shook her finger at us. "That stuff's bad for ya."

"OK," my brother and me said. And we'd stand there in the driveway with disappointed looks on our faces, watching the truck pass by. We'd look over our shoulders, to see if our mother was looking out the window to check on us. Finally we saw her do this, lingered for one more minute, then dashed to our bicycles, stashed on the side of the house, so we wouldn't have to open the garage door. Just in case, we rode in the opposite direction of the truck, went the long way around the block, and joined up with the cloud truck and the horde of kids following it over on Kings Road.

Everybody who was anybody on a bike was there. Choppers were all the rage in those days. Easy Rider had just come out a few years before, and spawned a plethora of biker flicks. The Hells Angels were still fairly new. And young. Every kid in these suburban neighborhoods fancied himself a biker on his Sting Ray or Mustang. All these little hard guys, these wanna-be motorcycle madmen riding around.....On bikes with crazy names. Lemon Peelers. Orange Crates. Iridescent yellow, orange and green bikes riding into the white clouds.

A lot of kids worked on their bikes, souped em up. They'd lengthen the curved front forks; stretch that front wheel out chopper-style. The Doyle family, a group of six brothers, were the forerunners in our neighborhood. One of em added two fork extensions, and attached a small lawn mower wheel out front. Super long forks with a super-small front wheel. Wild. Just like the handlebars. Big handlebars curved like ram horns. One kid had a steering wheel instead of handlebars. Others sported big banana seats, some raised ridiculously high, where the rider could hardly reach the pedals.

I remember riding into these billowing clouds that stretched high and wide, obscuring everything. An opaque white fog enveloped me. I can still remember the petroleum smell of the dense insecticide gas. Sometimes I'd hit a curb, or another bike, because I couldn't see a foot in front of me. But that was all part of the fun, riding blind, full-speed into the whirl of clouds.

Joey Sorbo, the baddest kid on a bike in the neighborhood, was there. He used to ride around looking for kids to run off the road. He'd do flying side-skids into smaller kids' bikes, or drive right at them on collision course, running kids off the road or making them wipe out. So everybody sort of edged away from him when he joined the pack of kids riding through the swirling haze. Everybody left him alone, gave him a wide berth, and he was free to ride as close as he could to the nozzle that sprayed out the clouds of DDT...... This guy is probably walking around glowing in the dark somewhere today, probably in one of those housing developments that gobbled up the woods where we used to play.

We could never have a time like that nowadays. Not with all these do-gooders running around trying to save everyone from everything. Second-hand smoke. Cholesterol. Too much sugar. Or caffeine. Helmets for kids on bikes now. Airbags. Smoke detectors. Security cameras. Everybody wants to be absolutely 100% safe from cradle to grave. They can't see what a precarious thing life is, no matter what you do.

Oh well. Maybe we knew better back then. My Mom knew we were playing in the DDT. "Ah, let 'em have a little fun," she probably figured. "It probly won't kill em." That's the way she thought back then. She still thinks like that. God bless her.

Yifter the Shifter

Mo Farah's recent repeat Olympic victories in the 5000 and 10,000 meters bring to mind great long distance runners of the past. One of them was Myrus Yifter, who won the 5000 and 10,000 meters in the same Olympics just once, not twice. And it was in the 1980 Moscow Olympics, boycotted by the West, so it didn't get much press. But Myrus was our track team's hero well before he even ran those two brilliant races.

I remember how it all started. We went to the Millrose Games, the premier event of the winter track season, held at New York's Madison Square Garden. Took the bus up from our hometown in New Jersey. Practically all the distance runners on the team were there. This kid Petry was our unofficial leader. He frequently went to the City on the train. So he was our guide, as we arrived at Port Authority and threaded our way through the crowd toward the Garden. We checked out the decaying 1970s New York scenery (half the place had that bombed-out ghetto look back then), accented by wisecracks from Petry.

Petry really hammed it up as our 'boss'. Like some people from New Jersey, he acted like he was in the Mafia. He even wore his varsity jacket on his shoulders, with his arms out of the sleeves, like one of the old Dons. He signaled us with nods of the head and subtle motions of the hands. He was a trip. And we were a colorful bunch heading to that track meet that night. There was Petry the tough guy, me the half-hippy, half jock, Silvers the intellectual, Benson the hustler and Tiocco the lady's man, plus others.

We headed to our seats. They weren't bad. We were about halfway up, and could see the track clearly. The hubbub of the crowd pressed in on us.

Petry perused his program, looking over the events and runners. His blue eyes got real big. "Hey—looka this guy in the 5000! Myrus Yifter! Fuckin Myrus! What a name!"

"Wonder what he looks like." I said. We looked down at the track, at the runners, and the numbers pinned to their jerseys. We looked for Myrus and his corresponding number

"There he is!" Petry pointed to a tall slender black man. He was bald up top, but sported a big Afro on the sides. And a big mustache.

"Check him out," I said.
"That's our man!" Petry yelled, excited.

We moved up from our seats, getting closer to the track. There are a lot of empty seats in a track meet in the U.S. We kept moving closer. By race time were near the edge of the track.

The runners, of all different nationalities, and with all different-colored uniforms, gathered at the starting line. We saw the half bald, half Afroed, mustachioed man take the track. "Yeah! Myrus!" We all yelled. "Go Myrus!"

Myrus glanced in our direction, a confused look on his face. I doubt he knew anybody from New York back then. It was early in his career.

"Yay Myrus!" We kept cheering. "Get 'em baby!"

The starting gun went off, and Myrus took off into the jumble of bodies.

"Hey looka that," Petry said. "He's near the head of the pack!"

I looked at him. Myrus was a tall muscular runner, with huge quads and calves He took long strides, arms level, hands open, a confident look on his face. "Hey, he's movin up!" Petry now called the race like an old-time horse-race announcer. "Holy shit! Now he's takin the lead!"

Myrus not only took the lead, he added to it, with those long, relaxed strides. He made it look easy. And it looked hard for the other runners. There was a strained quality to the way they ran.

"Aw right, Myrus!" We all shouted as he

ran past us, well in the lead with two laps to go. "look at him go!" Petry had to yell louder, over the increasing noise of the crowd.

The bell rang, signaling the last lap. The second and third place runners picked up the pace, looked like they had some ideas about catching up to Myrus.

Myrus had other ideas. He heard them, then took off like a rocket. That's how he got his nickname, Yifter the Shifter. He'd shift into overdrive when challenged. Meters stretched out between him and the rest of the pack. Still he poured it on more. He exploded down the home stretch, legs and arms pumping, teeth gritting, face strained. His chest broke the tape at the finish line, feet banging on the wooden boards of the indoor track. He won by a good ten meters.

He showed some class, too. He didn't stagger to the infield and just about collapse, like some runners (like me) would have done. He just walked it off, ambling down the track and catching his breath. He never looked back, I remember that.

"Yeah! My man!" Petry screamed.
"Yay, Myrus!" we all joined in. It was a great track moment.

After that, Myrus became our team hero. "I'm gonna run a Myrus-like race," I'd say before I ran the two-mile.

And if someone started giving up in practice, started taking it easy, we'd say, "Come on man, what would Myrus say?" We looked up to him for quite a while. A least a few seasons. And I'm still proud to read Myrus' name as the winner of the 5000 and 10,000 meters in those strange, "lost" Olympics in Moscow 1980.

Life, Death and Two Knuckleheads

"Hey, you nearly ready?"

"Yeah, I got one more cage to clean."

"Cool, I wanna get outta here."

"Hey did you see that cat in Ward 3? He's all fucked up."

"Yeah, why don't we check him out before we lock up?"

"OK….."

"…..Look at him."

"Ew, man."

"Doc says the only reason he's still alive is cause he landed in the grass."

"Looks like he's had it as it is."

"Again we see, flesh and blood is no match for the steel."

"That's for sure."

"He might make it."

"Come on, man. His jaw was sittin sideways on his head when he came in here."

"Yeah, but the Doc fixed that."

"Still. Look at him. He's got a broken front leg, busted ribs, a broken tail. Plus look, he ain't movin. He's probly still in shock."

"No he ain't. Look at his eyes, they're movin around a little."

"Yeah, but is he seeing anything? I think he's had it, man."

"I dunno, he might make it."

"Get a bag ready."

"Hey—fuck you! I oughta report you to the Doc, just for sayin that."

"Yeah, yeah report me."

"And another thing. The cat can hear ya."

"So what? He doesn't speak English."

"How do you know?"

"He speaks cat. If he speaks anything."

"Yeah, but it's the intent, brother. The intent is everything."

"Tttt. You are a true oddball. Are we ready to go?"

"Yeah, hit the lights, will ya? Poor little guy, I hope he makes it."

"I wouldn't bet money on it."

"I don't know, man. Look at his eyes."

"You and your eyes."

"You sure that's locked?"

"Yeah. Catch ya tomorrow."

"Hey looka that! He made it through the night!"

"Told ya. Look, I just seen him move!"

"Yeah right, he moved. He's layin there flatter than a pancake."

"But he made it through the night. That means he's gonna recover."

"I don't know. That might be a crackpot theory you have there."

"I'm tellin ya man, with cats, if they make it through the first night, they make it all the way."

"OK, how about that one cat in Ward One? Just last month. 'Member him, a big black cat. He lived through the night, but died a coupla days later."

"Yeah, but he had super-hyper kidney failure."

"Super-hyper?"

"You know what I mean. That cat was on his last legs when he got here."

"Yeah, but what about that silver tabby, got hit by the car last year?"

"Dude, he didn't make it through the first night."

"I thought he hung around for a couple of days."

"You kiddin? He got run over by a car, I mean the wheel went right over him, he didn't just bounce off a bumper, like our boy here. Nothin can make it through that. And besides, look at all the cats that made it after a rough first night. That one that came in here with distemper, he looked like history on the first night. But he made it all the way back. How about the other one, that got bit in the neck by a German Shepherd? Looked like he was a goner. But he made it back too. Think of all the other ones that looked like hell on the first night but went on to full recovery."

"Well, maybe ya got a point. But that is still one seriously mangalated animal."

"We'll see."

"Hey! He's up and around!"

"Get outta here!"

"Well, standing up anyway. Come check it out."

"Gimme a coupla minutes."

"OK....."

"....Look at that, up and at 'em!"

"Hey, he's trying to drink the water we left."

"But look, it's all runnin down the sides of his mouth."

"Some of it's going down."

"He does look a little bit better. He's not out of the woods yet, though."

"Always so negative."

"Realistic."

"Whatever."

"Hey, come and see our boy eating."

"I'm busy with this shit. Literally."

"Whoa! That looks pretty gross, man. Ya need a hand?"

"I got it. Two guys would make it worse. I'll come see ya when I'm done."

"Right...."

".....Hey he's eating the baby food, huh?"

"Yeah, look at him, chowin down like a champ!"

"I'm thinkin he's turned the corner. Eatin, that's big."

That's for sure. We'll see...."

"Ya see our boy today? He's up and about. Pacin the cage."

"Yeah, I did. When did he start eating regular catfood, anyway?"

"Oh, the last couple of days."

"Yeah, he does look better, a little. Did ya study last night?."

"Nope. Went to the bar."

"Hey, finals are just around the corner. And that biology's a bitch this semester."

"I got it. Keep trying to tell ya, I read the chapter before the lecture. Helps a lot."

"Okay…..."

"Ow! He had the claws out on that one!"

"Yeah, he's startin to play for real. Think the worm has turned for our boy."

"Think you might be right."

"'Member when he first came in? He couldn't move at all, remember? Now look at him. Runnin, jumpin, tryin to scratch us."

"He looks much better, I have to admit."

"Hey, guess who's going home today?"

"Not the Schofield cat in Ward 3?"

"None other. Mrs. Schofield is in the waiting room right now."

"Oh yeah? What's she look like?"

"Like a lot of the other women that come in here. Looks like somebody's mother, ya know?"

"Hmm. What? You're staring into space."

"I was just thinking....weird, ain't it? What lives and what doesn't?"

"That's for sure."

"Want to bring him out with me?"

"Yeah?"

"Yeah."

"Gimme a coupla minutes. I gotta finish up in here."

"I gotta brush him up anyway. I want our boy lookin good when he goes home."

www.ingramcontent.com/pod-product-compliance
Lightning Source LLC
Chambersburg PA
CBHW071128090426
42736CB00012B/2051